Life Forces a Journey

Jackie L. Disch

♦ JLD Publishing ♦
Minneapolis, Minnesota

To Katy -
   whose love, support, encouragement,
   understanding, and presence have
   brought new meaning to my life

In memory of Sara (1961-1999) -
   who continues to teach and guide me

Thank you -
   to everyone who helped in the
   creation of this book; may peace
   be with you and keep you well

Contents

Part III - Craziness is Just a Word

Part IV - Stray Bullets

Part I -

Child of Innocence

The Past Has Gone

The past has gone
     the future's near
The present's now
     what do you fear?

The questions asked
     the lies been told
Tell me now
     the truths you hold.

The mind can think
     the heart can feel
You know what's right
     but is it real?

The lights go out
     the night has come
The dreamer's dream
     is never won.

Child of Innocence

Once
 child of innocence
Time
 passed quickly
Suddenly grown
 into adulthood.
  Death of innocence
  Birth of maturity
Make way
 for responsibilities
No room
 for mistakes now -
  too old
  too soon.
Stolen
 secrets of youth
Washed away
 in a flood
of senility
 too old - too soon
  too late.
Child of Innocence
 has been murdered
By the childhood dream
 of wanting
  to grow
  up.

Darkness is Queen

Deep in the night
      where darkness is Queen -
you dare not question
her authority to rule.
Mystery, magic, and mayhem
can occur during her period.
But there is nothing majestic
      in her manner of rudeness
as she violently takes hold
      of my emotions
turning laughter into tears
      security to fear.
I become a slave to her majesty
She controls me
      as a puppet on a string.
She twists and pulls
      at my sanity
Haunting me - taunting me
Saying that tonight
I will become
      her lasting lover.
Caressing my soul
      with the promise of peace -
She pulls me near
Doing all within her power
      to hold me there beside her.
As time passes
      and morning approaches -
Daylight breaks her spell
      and I am free
        once more
But I know - come sunset -
I will again enter the Court
      where darkness is Queen
Deep in the night.

Mind-field

War has been declared
      only
I'm not sure
      who the enemy is.
Crawling cautiously
      on the ground
suddenly paralyzed by fear
too scared to move
afraid of blowing myself up
Dazed and alone
      I realize
I'm stuck
      in the middle
      of a
         mind-field.

Raindrops

Are raindrops
    like snowflakes?
Is each one different -
    unique?
Has anyone
    taken the time
        to find out?
Or
    are rainy days
        too depressing
    to search
    for a trifle
        thing
    such as
uniqueness.

Undertow

Columbus was wrong
the world is not round -
but rather
flat.
I know
for I have sailed
the stormy seas.
I have been close
      to the edge -
pulled near
by the undertow
yet held afloat
and at safety
by the upper current.
One of these days
      I'm going to go over
          the edge
splashing into
oblivion.
For now -
my head remains
above water
and filled
      with anxiety
of when the undertow
will grab me
      again.

Ignorance

If ignorance is bliss
then
stupidity must be a blessing.

Sea of Regret

I'm drowning in a sea of regret
remembering things I'd like to forget
      the past holds on
      like an autumn tree
         not ready to die
      And I sit here
         asking myself why
      I did the things I've done -
      and it seems I'm the only one
         that time won't heal
         those still open wounds
      and the present won't bury
         the feeling of doom
      that lurks behind each closed door
I don't think I can take anymore.
         But the days keep coming
            and soon they'll be gone
And I'll be sitting here rocking
         - still wondering -
where I went wrong.

Time

Time
   passes on
sometimes slowly
then
   it's gone
  moving on
past the day
  when you thought
   you had it made
But then
   time
    turns back the clock
to a period
        you forgot
  Except your mind
still remembers
      all those
slightly burning embers
  causing
time
  to go astray
losing more and more
each day
  Now you find
the years weren't kind
as you slowly
  lose your mind
and your clock
      runs out
  of
Time

Have a Nice Day

Can you promise me
       a tomorrow filled
            with joy?
Can you ensure me
       a tomorrow filled
              with laughter and love?
Can you guarantee me
       a tomorrow unlike
              today and yesterday?
I can no longer bear
the thought of carrying
all this pain with me
       forever.
I become weak at the thought
       of holding onto
              myself
              alone.
If you cannot
       make the promise
       or ensure me
or give me the guarantee
then at least smile
and tell me
       to have a nice day.

Suicidal Tendencies

You lay in bed at night
waiting for sleep to come
knowing it's not
all that easy.
Thoughts of yesterdays
flood your mind -
you start tossing
and turning
You close your eyes tighter
in an effort
to block the pain
the tears
from ripping you
apart.
You grab yourself
and hold on -
rocking back and forth
as fear, frustration
and eventually anger
start pounding
in your head.
A few external minutes pass
and the storm subsides.
You sigh deeply
wipe the tears from your face
and roll over
falling into a seemingly
gentle sleep
(if you are lucky - if not
the storm comes again
and you hold on once more).
Once you finally
fall to sleep
you wake up
again

and again
and again –
sometimes screaming
sometimes sweating
sometimes silent.

Miraculously
morning arrives
so you get up
(sometimes)
and face the new day.
In the mirror
you see the damage
of last night's storm/s
(and of those the
night before and
the night before) -
the deep dark circles
under your eyes
sunken cheeks
and most fearing -
the hollow
yet painful and weary
look in your eyes.
You made it through
another night
but can you make it through
another day?
Another day
of guilt and paranoia.
Another day
of the questions and lies.
Another day
of fake smiles
and polite conversations.
Another day
hating every

Goddamn minute stuck
with the same old
feelings and thoughts.
And then the
frustration sets in again
and the anger -
and you almost
beat the shit
out of someone
because they
looked at you wrong
or too long
or not long enough.
One minute you're laughing
the next close to tears.
You want to scream,
"Someone help me, please!"
But you know it's no use
The walls are
too thick
too high.
People see you slipping -
do what they can
sometimes
but what they offer
isn't enough
And you can't trust
them 'cause
they'll get you good
in the end.
You feel vulnerable,
used, stepped on,
stepped over, unwanted,
unloved.
Your tolerance
is getting lower
you don't care anymore.

At home
you feel alone,
lonely, empty...
you want to do nothing
yet something.
You reach for the telephone
but you know
you won't say anything
so you hang it back up
undialed.
You sit and stare
wondering
just what in the hell
you did to deserve it.
But you know
(oh - yeah - you know)
you were born
you're alive
you don't deserve to be here
you don't deserve to be.
Once again
you go to bed
completely exhausted
and wait for sleep to come
yet knowing
it's not all that easy
knowing you're within
one small step
of blowing up
going nuts
or killing yourself.
And why not?
You've felt like this
all or most of your life.
You're getting tired
of being confused
angry, frustrated

lonely - full of pain
hurt and hate...
fearing death
as much as life.

Silence is Golden

Silence is golden
    but where is the pay?
No wisdom be known
    if no one can say!
But all is not spoken
    if all is not said
So words that are written
    must surely be read.
For those who dare
    to defy quiet roles
Tomorrow will show us
    our payment in whole.
As the silence is broken
    then all unknown pains
Shall be known to all
    bringing freedom again!

The Starting of Romance

A risk
  a chance
a sigh
  a glance
a signal
  an advance
The starting
  of romance

A want
  to share
A need
  to care
Someone
  is there
to love -
  beware

An end
  can come
before
  the fun
is truly
  done
One starts
  to run

A laugh
  a cry
A risk
  a sigh
A chance
  to try

too late
  good-bye

Someone to Hold

I want someone
    to show my soft
        side to.
I want someone
    I can gently touch -
    someone to hold on to.
I want someone
    to love me
I want someone to love.

Lost Loves

I have loved
And I have lost those loves
Happiness turned into bitterness
Boredom replaced excitement
Trust gave way to jealousy
Laughter became an unknown element
        leaving only tears to flow
And time spent alone
        began feeling better
than time spent together

Love was no longer joy
        but had metamorphosed
            into pain

If It's All the Same to You

If it's all the same to you
    I'll stay
in summer's green
    not winter's gray
For love turns cold
    as does the wind
and may grow too old
    to begin again.

If it's all the same to you
    I'll stay
where lover's hearts
    aren't in dismay
Where youthful smiles
    fill naïve faces
taking their dreams
    to far away places.

If it's all the same to you
    I'll stay
in silent wonder
    of today
For love has found me
    once again
as if to answer
    where it's been.

Part II -

Movement

If You Saw Me

You wouldn't know me
if you saw me
and you wouldn't see me
if you knew

A Leaf on a Tree

Once
    I was a leaf
    hanging on a tree
Then
    someone came along
    and plucked me.

She held me
    in her hand
as she walked
    down the street
Then I was dropped
    on the ground
and stepped on
    by her feet.

Crazy Woman

Words
run around in my head
pretend
to really *be* something
mean something.
Mostly
they just get dizzy
because they run
in a circle
waiting for my mouth
to open
so they can jump out.
By that time
they've run around
in a circle
all their lives
So naturally
they come out
all twisted.

Childhood Revisited

I am a child again.
All the years
    of feeling an adult
have filtered to
    this point
The point of being free
    to laugh
        play - explore
The freedom to feel
    hurt
    anger - pain
I am here at last
at my childhood
    which never existed
which was never allowed
which I never claimed.

Swallowed

I feel as though
I'm being swallowed
by blackness
which is seeping
from within
and overcoming me.
I am inside
reaching out -
feeling desperate
in my struggle
    to survive.

Solitude Deepens

My solitude deepens
my pain increases
        in intensity.
Death does not claim
        to be the only
        way to stop
        the pain
simply the quickest.

My inner soul sinks
deeper into
        depression.
My outer voice
is weak
        in protest.

My struggle is not
to live or die -
rather, it is in
how to end the pain.

What I Want

What I want
is for someone
to be able to
reach inside
and help me
    heal.

I Am

I am haunted by
shadows
    images
vague memories
threatening to push through
the outer limits
    of my soul.

I am
    blocking
        fighting
            forcing
the thoughts back down
        to a quiet place…
not calm
not peaceful
        just quiet.

I am avoiding
    the knowledge
that is already known.
I am averting my eyes
    from visions
I have already seen.

In my desperate need
    to believe
in my present reality,
    I am denying
        the existence
            of my past.

If I Could

If I could voice
    the anger
in my heart

If I could release
    the tears
of my pain

If I could see
    the years
of my isolation

Then I would speak
    the secrets
of my soul

Beyond

Beyond the struggle
    to merely exist
is the desire
    to survive.

Honesty Denied

The honesty I lack
is the truth I deny

Encouragement

Beyond the shadow
    of a doubt
Behind the eye
    of the beholder
beauty will be found -
And like a seed
    planted deeply
it will take root
      and grow
soaring
from the nurturing words
    of encouragement

Tears Drop

Tears
roll down my face
not knowing
why they are there
they simply do
as they are told
and fall

Movement

Understand
the truth
Recognize
the shame
Only then
is it possible
To move
forward

Logical Equation

Sometimes
it is difficult
    to put two and two
together
    and end up with four.
The logical equation
becomes a struggle
and somehow
    even the even numbers
come out odd.

Wordlessly

Wordlessly
we touch
one another
far deeper
than this
reality allows

Part III -

Craziness is Just a Word

Shame

I seem to be caught
in a cesspool of shame.
The shame revolves around
some of my other feelings.
The shame is internalized
from the past
and can paralyze me to inaction.
The shame and my biggest wound
are intimately connected.
It is the wound
that often gets bumped up against -
the wound that I
have always tried to ignore
or protect against -
the wound that makes
my stomach churn
or makes me recoil
when I get too close to it myself.
The wound
is my biggest secret
and my biggest secret
is covered with shame.
Both the wound and the shame
cause me pain –
so that it becomes extremely difficult
to touch
or heal
either.

I Can't See

I want to write
but can't seem to find
what I want to say.
I need to cry
but my eyes remain dry.
I want to feel
whatever it is
that has my soul reeling.
But my head
and my heart
seem miles apart.
And my feelings
and their words
are not on speaking terms.
And I can't seem to touch myself
in any deep way –
though I know
I feel a lot
deeply.
It's all off a beat
or the connection is lost -
disconnected
or misdirected
or maybe not.
Could be that everything
is just how it should be
even if I can't see.

Stepping Over

Let the darkness fall around me
let it seep into my soul
let it take me from the present
to a place I do not know.

Let the silence end its ruling
let it step down off the throne
let it go where voice is hidden
to speak words I've never known.

Let the pain I'm in release me
let it forgive me of my sin
let it force me to step over
to a place I've never been.

Reconstruction

I just want
to crawl inside myself
so that the pain
and I am one.
The struggle
would then be over
and I would know
what it's like
        to *feel*.

The Breaking of Day

I want to go
    where the edge of the clouds
        meet the breaking of day...
    where the horizon shows promise
        of an easier time...
    where I can release my struggles of today
        and find a purpose for tomorrow...

I Wish I Could Say

I wish
I could say
more to you
than I do

On guard -
protective
of my own
limitations
and yours

I can only say
what is safe
for either of us
to hear

which leaves me silent

with only a wish
that I could say
more to you
than I do

Evil Considered

You can do bad things
and not be evil.
You can do good things
and be evil as hell.

Please Do Not Touch Me

Please do not touch me.
It hurts, sometimes,
much more than
never being touched at all.

A touch can bring
all the hidden pain
to the surface
where it becomes
impossible to deny.
A touch can send
the sense of caring
deep into my core
where caring before
had been dangerous.
A touch can set in motion
a flood of feelings
that is overwhelming
and scary.

So please do not touch me.
It hurts,
much more than
never being touched at all.

Medication Time

Medicate your fears
drink a few more beers
move into a state
of numbness
Where there are no laws to break
you just get what you can take
and leave the rest
behind you.

Depression

Depression had lifted
its dreary head
I had hoped it was gone
for good, but instead
I've found it has deepened
in new ways now known -
it feels like a cancer
in the marrow of my bones -
it spreads like a fire
through the blood in my veins -
and through it all
I try to be sane.

But depression fights dirty
and the more I fight
the harder it is to tell
what's wrong or what's right -
and so the struggle continues
depression still ahead -
in this game we are playing
I may end up dead.

Craziness is Just a Word

Am I really crazy?
Does anybody know?
If I could conceal it
and never let it show,
then maybe I could convince myself
and everyone else around
that craziness is just a word
that doesn't make a sound.

Sweet Sorrow

Sweet sorrow pass the plate
I'll have two servings of self-hate.
I'll eat off the table of evil and sin
Then starve myself till I begin again.

Sadness Seeps

Sadness
seeps
into my
soul
telling me
something
I don't
know
how to
let you
help me
please
before
these visions
that I see
consume
and
destroy
me

But I Was Afraid

I wanted to walk in
and have you hold me.
Sometimes, being held
is the best way to touch
      what is healing.

But I was afraid.
Had I asked,
would you have said no?
Or think badly of me?

Shame still
exposes my need
and keeps me quiet
      in my pain.

An Island

An island
     caught
between the sky
  and sea
Water surrounding
as far as the eye
  can see
There is no
     ship to shore
  anymore
Seagulls dance
  above the waves
     and tide
No place on land
  where a soul
can hide
Deserted,
     alone,
abandoned - not free
An island
     caught
between the sky
  and sea

Quiet Solitude

In the sometimes
quiet solitude
of my room
I wonder if
I'm going crazy
or if
I'm already
there.

Part IV -

Stray Bullets

Your Will

I will withhold my feelings
I will withhold
I will
I will withhold my anger
I will withhold my love
I will withhold my disapproval
I will
I will withhold
I will withhold
I will withhold my relationship with you
I will withhold my relationship
I will withhold
I will withhold to punish
I will withhold to protect
I will walk away
I will withhold
I will swallow all of my rage
I will withhold
I will swallow all of my joy
I will
I will swallow
I will wallow
I will deny
I will regret
I will wish you wrong
I will withhold
I
I will withhold
I will reject me
I will project you
I will
I will wish me harm
I will blame me
I will withhold
I will behold

I will be held
I will with
I will hold
I will
I will withhold you
I
I will
I will withhold without being told
You hold with will,
me.

Seeing and Believing

If seeing is believing
must you believe
in order to see?

Dead People

She says to me,

"What are we going to do
with all these dead people?"

And an image pops into my head -
I want to ask if she often sees
dead people.

I smile,
laughing to myself, refrain from asking my question.
She is talking about
the people in our lives who have died,
what happens to them?
I tell her I'll write a poem about that.

One thing about dead people
is they don't stay dead.
They walk the halls of our memories,
enter our dreams,
and are embedded
in the sights,
sounds, and smells
of our lives.
They haunt us
or comfort us
or keep us company when we are lonely.
They can make us laugh
cry
or sigh with contentment
with whichever thought
happens by in the breeze.

Some religions teach
that the soul leaves the body upon death

and goes to heaven or hell –
or some variation on that theme.
Karma teaches us
that the "person" will come back
to continue her or his work.

Some people bury the dead in the ground
then try to forget they had lived.
Some bury themselves in the ground with the dead
and try to forget they are still alive.
Still others hold onto the love and life
that was shared with the one who died
and try to fill or heal the hole
that is left in their lives.

Some can only sit and stare,
wondering "why."

Others don't have a clue
what happens to the dead person
and don't even bother to ask –

"What are we going to do
with all these dead people?"

Send them on their way, I say –
wherever that may be!
And if it is someone
you really love,
hope that your paths will cross again

in whatever way
in whatever shape
in whatever form that may be.

Counting Snowfalls

I watch as they talk
among themselves
A private conversation
in a public place.
I am there, sitting with them
It appears I am a part of
the conversation
But there is an invisible wall
between us all –
me on one side
them on the other –
that sets me a-part-from
the conversation instead.
I smile and nod, trying
to be involved
But their lips form words
telling me little about themselves
or their lives,
although they appear to
be saying something more
substantial.
      She bet these many
      He bet that
A disagreement ensues
      then laughter –
Her husband has lost track.
They are counting snowfalls,
making bets on the final outcome.
It is a new way to talk about the weather,
which is an old way of making polite
conversation.

Spent Offerings

I offer no explanation
no excuses.
I stand naked
     vulnerable.
I will not defend myself
   against
       attack
       criticism
       or admiration.
I will not speak.
Will not spin a web of words
   to comfort
   or contort myself.
You may judge me
      analyze me
      commend me
      condemn me
      praise me
      or dismiss me.
Still I will stand
   speechless
   defenseless
   silent
         Surrendered.

Below the Cut

I've just been informed
my eligibility ranking is
below the cut

Below the cut

What a cutting blow
didn't make the grade
I try to take my assets
out of the line of fire
but the news cuts deep
into my reserve
of self-esteem

Below the cut

Cuts you off from others
places them above you
ranked in order
filed in line
One, two, three, four
Sorry
only have room for
one more

Below the cut

There's something
very demeaning
about that phrase
Removes you from the race
Couldn't cut it
- Cut it out -

Below the cut

Cuts below the surface
hitting the fluff
I am suddenly made of
A cut below the rest
Several layers removed
from the best

Below the cut
Hurts like the cut
that it is
Jabbing, stabbing
little blow
to my ego

Below the cut

A blow below the belt
It's hard not to be reduced
to your score on a test of Nothing
when that nothing puts you
below the cut.

Looking Back

I look back
through my mama's eyes
see her life
and mine
in a manner
only time allows.

I walk back
through the years
thinking
surely she must
see things now –
surely she must *know* –
surely she can no longer think
that life was
any different
than it was.

What seemed right at the moment
couldn't possibly look right now.
What was wrong at the time
couldn't possibly be seen
any other way now.

Regrets
Mistakes
I imagine my mother
pouring over them all
in her mind.
Worrying
Fretting
trying to figure out
how to make it right.
Fearful that she can't
Faintly hopeful that she can.

I imagine her
looking back at her life,
seeing some of the things she's done
and wondering how on earth
she could have done them
or let them happen.
Realizing
if she had it all to do over again
she *would* do it differently.

Possibly even wishing for the chance.

I picture my mother
slowly grasping the impact
she has had on my life
And as that understanding dawns on her
she reaches back
through time
wanting desperately
to change it.

But I know
it's only child's play.
Magical thinking
is the only thing
that lets me look back
through her eyes.
And when I do
I see what I want her to see,
the way I want her to see it.

I can't look back
through my mama's eyes.
But maybe
I can get her to look back
through mine.

Tender Memory

It is tender
when I touch that memory.
I would rather not go there.
But my mind seems to return to it
Time and time again.
Or maybe it is the memory
that reaches out
and touches my mind
sending a wave of shock
and panic
through the rest of my body.

It is tender
when I touch that memory.
My stomach clutches
into a tight ball,
nausea rumbling through.
I mentally stop myself
from throwing up
only slightly aware
that doing so is a betrayal
to my body –
it wants to puke
but I won't let it.

It is tender
when I touch that memory.
My throat tightens
    trying to hold in a scream?
    the story?
It's hard to tell which.
It's hard to tell.
Now, fire burns my throat
as if holding it all in
creates a friction

so intense
that it rubs my throat raw.

It is tender
when I touch that memory.
Every nerve in my body
snaps to attention.
Fear races through me
chased by anxiety
propelled by panic.
I want to run from it all
but there is no place to go.

It is tender
when I touch that memory.
Shame covers me
protects me
so that I don't have
to talk about it.
Shame moves in
so that I can push
the memory
and all its pain and sorrow
        out
                away
until the next day
or the next minute
or the next wave
brings it flowing back to me.

It is tender
when I touch that memory.
An ache fills my heart
like a deep bruise
        tender to the touch
        tender to the brush

of the memory
up against it.

It is tender
when I touch that memory.
I would rather not go there
But I do.

Slumber

It is a wall
That deep within
No other one
Can touch or feel

An empty void
A blank slate
Upon which
My fate is drawn

It slumbers now
This hideous scar

Scar Tissue and Abrasions

My body remembers
what my mind does not want.
Still, I see and know
and I imagine
what it would be like
to live through it all again.
I can feel it happening,
though it is removed enough
so that only twinges touch
my real body now.
I wonder
how can I release you
so that my body, mind and soul
may heal?
What do you need from me?
What do you need?
If I could reach inside
and touch the parts of my body
that were injured,
I would.
I would take them in my hands
- into my arms, if I could -
massaging the wounds
stitching and sewing
the tears and shreds,
restore normal breathing,
stop the bleeding, bring renewed balance
to the brain and body.
I would hold and comfort
and talk, until the fear quelled.
I would mourn
the attack, the casualties it brought.
I would grieve the loss
and ease the pain.
I would defend and protect

from another attack –
giving time for the raw
ripped-open wounds
to heal.

I would reach in
and touch myself
the way I couldn't then,
lovingly tending
to the brutal results
so scar tissue
and abrasions
would never have to form,
and decades later
my body would not need to remember
what my mind does not want.

She Is

I protect her
I suppose
like I protect
no other.
She sits alone
         away
from everyone else.
She
is the keeper
of my feelings.
She is
Lonely
She is
Sad
She is
Angry
She is
Hurt
She is
Alone.
She
is isolated,
tucked away
from all to see
and hear
and know.
She is where
my feelings go
when I cannot stand
to have them –
when I don't know
what to do with them –
when it seems
safer
better

wiser
for whatever reason –
healthy or not –
to keep them away
from me.

I almost
can't reach her now.
She's been too far away
for too long.
It feels like
she's dying
now.

Stray Bullets

I still flinch
when it flashes
Still duck
from the view
Don't want the impact
of the impact
to sever me in two.
Try hard
to dodge the bullets
this memory slings
my way
But always
I move too slowly
and am shattered
by a stray

Ungrounded

"I am Jackie here and now."
>But I feel a tug
>trying to pull me away

"I am Jackie"
>my mind wanders

"here and now"
>no I'm not, I think.

Deep breath
Focus

"I am Jackie here and now."
>No. I'm not. I try but
>I don't believe it.

"I am Jackie here and now."
>Whenever I say that
>I feel a presence.
>It does not want me to be
>Jackie here and now.

Try again
Deep breath
Focus

"I am Jackie here and now."
>I wonder why it doesn't want me to be
>Jackie here and now
>But I only wonder
>I don't ask.

"I am Jackie here and now."
>I try to ignore not being
>Jackie here and now
>but I can't.
>Still, I am avoiding
>direct conversation.

"I am Jackie"
>there it is again

"here and now."
I force myself

to finish the mantra.
Pulled by the presence,
I look at it closer,
out of the corner
of my minds eye.
I give up trying to say it.

I *am* Jackie here and now –

aren't I?

Responsibility Denied

I cannot fix for you
everything that is wrong

I am not the problem
nor the cure

Your loneliness
your fear
your emptiness
your depression
your anxiety
are all yours.

Your desire to have me there
wrapped around your neck
like some warped security blanket
is nothing less than
another way to avoid
what belongs to you.

I cannot save you from yourself
I cannot save you from your past
I cannot comfort you
for the pain you caused me
I cannot ease it, erase it
ignore it, deny it
or make it go away
by any other means.

The guilt is yours
The discomfort is yours
The pain is yours
The anger is yours
The fear is yours
The depression is yours.

I cannot absorb it
like a sponge
thereby absolving you
of your own shit.

Like much of the past
you have created between us,
it is not my responsibility.

Emotional Bends

My heart is breaking
from the pain.
My soul is bleeding,
cracked open again.
The depth, it scares me
where my memory descends.
And crawling all through me
are the emotional bends.

Long Distance Running

I feel like going
      and going
        and going
wheels moving
beneath my feet –
miles rushing
through my Being
until all of the cobwebs
are cleared out of my head,
obstinate infectious remnants
are obliterated from my body,
leaving my injuries behind
in a potentially futile attempt
to out-distance
the pain.

Part V -

After Effects

Defiant

There is a sadness
that resides
within.
The further away I try to

                         push it

the more it hunkers down,
crouched on its haunches -
like a two year old
daring me to try and make it
move…

             Go ahead. I dare ya!

mouth turned down
eyebrows furrowed
arms tightly crossed

Defiant
yet dependent upon me.

I can no more turn by back
on my sadness
than I could a two year old child.

Problem Feeling

I'm having problems
with my feelings
because they are
pre-verbal
pre-consciousness
pre-ability to know
            what feelings are
            and how they feel

Can't name them
even if I know I have them
Don't know what they are
even if I feel them
Can't feel them
even when they are there

Post-fragmented
pile-up
of unexpressed,
unknown,
unidentifiable
                feelings

Identity Reclaimed

I am afraid of losing
who I have become.
Or maybe
I am afraid of becoming
who I have
lost.

Holding Back

I work at deep breaths, sighing
My chest is tight
My stomach flutters
My heart aches

Mad as hell
I am swallowing the feelings
that I don't know how
to let out,
choking on words
I won't let myself
speak
Afraid of the consequences

Always afraid of the consequences

You Can Ask (I Will Not Tell)

You can ask me how I am
and I will not tell you.
Not the truth.
I keep the truth as hidden from myself
as I do from you
or others, so no one can see.
But if you want a glimpse inside
then I will tell you of my pain
of my clandestine shame
of my anger and fearfulness
my helplessness and despair.
I will tell you how it is that I keep thinking
I should be in the hospital to keep myself safe
and yet I cannot say those words out loud.
I will tell you how empty I feel
how meaningless I am
and how lost I seem to have become again.
I will tell you that I wonder
how it is that I still function
when the feelings are so raw and strong
that I wonder how I can keep so much in
without others knowing what is going on
and I wonder what would happen if I told.
I can fill you in on my desire to run
to leave the pain behind
and that I know I would leave
the happiness behind too, so I stay.
I can tell you I feel overwhelmed
by my own silence
and become afraid of what will happen to me
if I don't talk
and that I am already afraid
of what is happening to me –
I feel out of control, or like I'm losing control
and I imagine myself forever trapped

in what I do not say
eventually pushing myself to insanity.
I can tell you there is a part of me
that wants to reach out – scream out –
all of these things to another human being
so that I am not alone in my pain
or in my struggles
So that someone else *knows*
what is going on.

But I do not say any of this
because I do not want to be a bother or a burden,
a disappointment or "dead weight."
So you can ask me how I am
and I will not tell you
because the truth and I
are concealed inside.

Nonsense or Necessary

Should I be able
to just pull myself
out of this?

Should I be able
to just stop
all this pain and sadness -

And just be happy
and enjoy life?

Should it be that simple
Is it entirely my fault (if it's *not* that simple)
Do I lack the control
Is the decision mine
Can I just "snap out of it"
And "stop all this nonsense"
Is it nonsense to others
Do they wish I would stop it
Do they think I can
With just a-wish-a-way?

Or is it necessary
And out of my hands –
A part of my journey
through grief.

Difficulty Breathing: A Realization

I take a deep breath
that I don't think
I deserve to take.

As I release
more and more
of the toxicity of my past,
I live
in a cleaner present –
breathing pure oxygen
rather than
pure bullshit.

As I begin to take
a deep breath
of this clean, fresh air
I stop,
hesitating
questioning
- do I deserve to take this breath?

Sometimes the mechanics
of my body take over
and complete the breath,
leaving the question hanging
in thin air.

Other times
I have difficulty breathing,
the deep breath
snatched away in mid-hale
as I realize
I am now anxious
about being able
to breathe so freely.

Natural Breakdown

Nature has a way
of bringing you back
to a primitive state.
Limited distractions
produce a natural
increase in awareness.
You notice the silence,
the pitch of the darkness
without city lights
to illuminate the night.
And all the things
you can usually run away from
finally catch up to you.
Slowly, day by day,
hour by hour,
minute by minute,
your feelings –
your fears and insecurities
your doubts and concerns
will surface
in one way or another.
Maybe not all of them
but at least one or two –
maybe you already know of them
maybe you don't.
But nature has a way
of breaking you down
so that your vision
is clearer –
and if you are fortunate -
your insights are deeper
and you won't run back
to the distractions
of your everyday life
to hide.

What is The Truth?

The truth is something
most people do not want to know
about themselves
about others
about a situation.
The truth
is something to hide,
cover until it
simmers
and boils.
The truth
is not always pleasant,
not always pretty,
sometimes not as ugly
as it could be
often more ugly than
it should be.
The truth
never comes and goes
or sways in the wind.
It always *is*
no matter what.
It does not decay
erode away
or get washed down stream
in the storm.
It stands stronger than anything,
man-made or natural.
Even a lie
cannot change the truth

It only makes the truth
harder to find.

The Garden Got Planted This Year

I didn't know
if it would happen.
The patch of ground lay untilled –
a rectangle of dirt,
like an open sore waiting
for life - or death
to claim it.

I spun a story in my head that said
Without him,
she will not go on.
Death has a way of changing life.
It alters the course of those who still live
in ways unexpected.
Even though we all know
that death is inevitable,
we remain blind to the changes it brings
until it has already passed
through.

I imagined her to grow frail,
the house put up for sale,
or for both of them to crumble and decay.
I imagined the garden patch
would remain unplanted
and overcome
with the weeds of abandonment.

I hear it was unexpected.
I saw the ambulance take him away
early one morning,
but he was sitting up.
Can't be too serious, I thought.
He'll be back in no time.
But he didn't return

and I couldn't help but wonder
what happened.
I couldn't imagine him dead.
Then I heard, as we moved toward spring,
that he had died
very unexpectedly.

I was stunned,
the suddenness overwhelming me.
He was so active.
And this past winter they stayed here
for the first time in years –
no longer traveling south for the season.
And now he is dead.
Last time I saw him he was walking up the hill
going to mail a letter or a bill, perhaps.

Since then, I have been watching and waiting –
projecting my own pain and loss
onto a woman I do not know except in passing.
I cry now and then –
a slight stream of tears run down my face
in response to what I think *she* must be feeling.

Each time I would look at my neighbors' house
I'd feel an unbearable twinge.
Tragic. Unnecessary.
I didn't know how I would bear her loss.
Occasionally, eventually,
I would see her moving around –
amazed at her strength, her agility.
She even began doing some of the things
he used to do.

Then one evening as I walked to my car,
I saw her standing outside near the garden.
A man had a tiller going

and he was working the ground.
My heart leapt,
surprising me with its delight.
The garden would be planted this year!
I felt an unknown burden ease,
the significance of the garden only then
revealing itself to me –
Life
not death
would claim it.

I Wonder if She Knows

I wonder if she knows
I saw her daughter
just before she died.
I am pretty sure it was she.
They drove by as we waited to cross the street.

The face in the passenger side window
        stood out
as though framed by fate for me to see.
I tried not to look,
tried not to invade their privacy.

But the moment I saw her
I thought that is was her daughter.

I was taken aback.
It struck me that the Universe
was showing her to me that day,
wanted me to see her for some reason.

She died some time between
that Friday and Monday.
I wonder how she died.
I wonder when.

I still see her face
framed by the window
frozen in time.

I wonder if she has
any idea how much
I have been touched
by her daughter's death.

Asking Forgiveness

If I knew then
what I know now
I would not have acted
as I had then –
But based on
what I do know now
I could not have acted
any other way.
Please forgive me.

Like a Name on The Wall

I look at your name
listed as a death
that has occurred in the last thirty days.
Like a name on The Wall
or a tombstone
I stare at it,
trying to figure out what it means.
How did you become letters
trapped on my computer screen?
I look
and your death
doesn't get any more real.
Or maybe it is too real
already.

After Effects

Death amazes me
and astounds me

leaves a void
that is bigger
than the person
who died

but is left
by that person
nonetheless.

I Can't Imagine (Tomorrow)

Tomorrow I attend the memorial service
of a good friend.

What in the hell am I doing?
I shouldn't have to!

I shouldn't have to.

It will be hard.
Accepting that she is dead is hard.

Tomorrow, I say goodbye to
to a good friend.

I'm sure I will cry.
I can't imagine not crying.

I can't imagine.

Life Forces a Journey

Life rarely goes in the direction
you think it is or isn't
or shouldn't or should.
It takes unexpected turns
that leave
unexpected burns –
on your psyche
on your soul,
what once was filled
there's now a hole.
Then you find yourself sitting
on a picnic table bench
trying to make sense
of yourself or your life
or the turn you took last night
or the thought you had a moment ago
when you thought you knew
where you had to go
or you thought your life
was going along fine
until you hit this crack in the road
that twisted your spine
and it made you turn to look
and see
you are not where you thought you were
and suddenly
you begin to think of your life again
where it's going and where it has been
and the past and the present
and the future converge
on this bend in the road
called "dead man's curve"
or maybe it's blind
and I just can't see
what's in front, to the sides,

or behind me —
even though I thought I knew where I was
descending upon me is this giant buzz
of questions unanswered
and lessons unlearned
about the direction of life
and its unexpected turns
and I'm trying to avoid
those burns that it gives
as it twists and it scrapes
and it rattles and digs
going down a new path
or some times an old
as Life forces a journey
that carves its own road.

Life Forces a Journey Order Form

Use this convenient order form to order additional copies of
Life Forces a Journey

Please Print:

Name_____

Address_____

City_____ **State**_____

Zip_____

Phone(**)**_____

      _____ copies of book @ $12.95 each $ _____
Postage and handling @ $ 3.50 per book $ _____
Add $1.75 for each additional copy
MN residents add 6.5% tax $ _____
Total amount enclosed $ _____

Make checks payable to JLD Publishing
P.O. Box 24231
Minneapolis, MN 55424

Watch for the JLD Publishing web page, coming soon.